Bibliographic information published by the German National Library:

The German National Library lists this publication in the National Bibliography; detailed bibliographic data are available on the Internet at http://dnb.dnb.de .

Imprint:

Copyright © 2006 GRIN Verlag, Open Publishing GmbH
Print and binding: Books on Demand GmbH, Norderstedt Germany
ISBN: 9783656734161

This book at GRIN:

http://www.grin.com/en/e-book/279756/importance-and-functions-of-communication

Teddy Kimathi

Importance and Functions of Communication

GRIN Publishing

GRIN - Your knowledge has value

Since its foundation in 1998, GRIN has specialized in publishing academic texts by students, college teachers and other academics as e-book and printed book. The website www.grin.com is an ideal platform for presenting term papers, final papers, scientific essays, dissertations and specialist books.

Visit us on the internet:

http://www.grin.com/

http://www.facebook.com/grincom

http://www.twitter.com/grin_com

IMPORTANCE AND FUNCTIONS OF COMMUNICATION

BY

TEDDY KIMATHI

IMPORTANCE AND FUNCTIONS OF COMMUNICATION

Communication is a very important tool, which has helped every one of us to co-exist with each other peacefully and happily. Without it, this world would not have become as it is today, due to several qualities and factors, which it possesses. Communication has been made possible due to some important factors.

First, in order to know the state of individual especially mental, emotional and psychological states Since the creation of this world, man has always survived and encountered many problems, which have been reduced by creating a bond or a relationship with his fellow being. Hence through speaking out his problem which heals or heals faster, he creates an intimate relationship which is caused by communication. For instance, psychologists have been successful in treating most of their patient because of grabbing a feeling of empathy inside their hearts. Lecturers, teachers and patients have also been successful because of creating a bond between them and the audience. For parents, affection, compassion and understanding have helped them too.

Secondly, it has helped in spreading up and improving business transactions. With today's technology devices have been invented which have made it possible to solve various problems in many transfer, banking and policing of services. This great equipment include; computers, tale-fax and telex and mobile phones. Computers have really helped in controlling money intake and withdrawing from banking. They have also really helped in securing business records of various companies and institutes. Telefax and telex have blessed businessmen with faster and more effective means of sending and receiving messages from other business oriented companies and businessmen. Mobile phones have also made work easier, for anyone can carry them anywhere; they are light and also convenient.

Thirdly, in the health sector, people, doctors and scientists have learnt more about courses and ways of preventing various diseases, their cure and treatment of certain injuries that are very prone to infection. The number of people going to hospitals and clinics has greatly reduced for the past few years, because of mere awareness about their health status with great contribution from booklets, seminars, films, books and magazines offered by doctors and researchers. Due to awareness, most of the Africa countries have battles police, Ebola and Whooping cough. AIDS the killer virus has also been revealed all over the world, hence people learning more about abstinence from sex till marriage and also sharing of needles, blades and toothbrushes.

Scientists have also been able to learn more about the natural and artificial threats to man. With the discovery of more advanced machines which send their own signals, scientists have unearthed great mysteries which took man centuries to discover and research. Earthquake, for instance is a natural and artificial threat to man, which has stopped to worry people because of the seismography, which records the rate of the earth's vibration from the ground. Satellites have helped scientists to predict earlier storms and droughts. Super-telescopes have helped scientists to know the state and balance of space, with relation to earth's security. Meteorites and asteroids are known for falling down on earth's surface.

In transportation, movement of people and goods has been made safer and less time consuming. Today's modern transportation vassals have been computerized, hence risks of getting accidents or things stolen, have been greatly reduced. For instance, comptrollers use satellites to know and establish the position which the plane, rockets, ships and submarines are located. From the satellites in space, signals are transmitted to the satellite boosters on the comptrollers departments, finally ending up to their computers, which show the information in form of images, codes and words. In the side of road transportation, road signs, vehicle computers and radios, have helped drivers to drive their vehicles more carefully without colliding with other vehicles or pedestrians. Signals are transmitted from the satellites to these communication devices in the vehicles, showing the drives the direction, location and situation which their vehicles are in.

It has also helped the underdeveloped areas to get access to information from the rest of the world. Due to lack of exposure to the outside world, some remote areas have suffered insecurity, health risks and poverty, due to lack of enough knowledge about the rest of the world. But with the help of radios, advisers and   computers, people have learnt more about means in which they can develop their areas and make their lives better. Radio for instance has really helped to shape the political, social and economic ideas, in the minds of the people. Through just learning the news a resident of a particular village can get the whole picture of who, where and what is being talked about. On the side of computers, various remote institutions have been able to get access to information, where newspaper and magazines can't reach. In Somalia for example, one can browse for any information that is in the newspaper.

On the side of guidance and counseling, woman and children have been advised on means of protecting themselves from various diseases and ailments, family planning and negativities of female genital mutilation. Various projects like digging of bore-holes, building stores and sanitation structures have been made possible with the help of domestic and foreign advisers.

As the main foundation to the press, communication has molded the political landscape of countries. In general, citizens of various countries have finally got an opportunity and a way of expressing their feelings or attitudes towards a particular way in which a country is governed. With the help of the newspaper and mass media, almost everyone is the world has come to realize his or her own limits, nights and freedom. For hundreds of years, demonstrations and civil wars have gained no fruit in removing dictators and bad monarchs from the seats of leadership. With time, people decided to use newspapers and radios to communicate to their leaders, expressing their feelings and thoughts. The first press was just in form of simple companies, which gradually grew to be in form of simple companies, which gradually grew to be re-known internationally.

In terms of education, it has enlarged the world of intellect. By just looking at the intellectual level of Africa, we will come to realize that the early Christian missionaries and colonial administration had done a bit in trying to sweep the whole carpet, which was filled with illiteracy. For more than one hundred and fifty years ago, Africans first got their education through reading and writing. After colonization of most Africans states, the Europeans brought in their academic books and instruments, which later and made Africans to evolve intellectually. Not only in Africa that education had been introduced by Europeans, but also in the Americas, some parts of Asia and Australia and New Zealand.

Looking at religion, it has been used as music and sermons, which have been carried on in churches, mosques, temples and synagogues, in order to attract new converts and create a spiritual atmosphere and peaceful moment for the mind. Sermons and creeds have been used by preachers and Imams to show and express God's intentions to the congregation or crowd. For many centuries, Christianity has thrived because of availability of texts and scriptures, which gave Christians a guideline on how they would live a peaceful and successful life, without using war and scientific theories as the wise means of creating a united world, which knows only one God. Since the time of the Jihads in Europe, crusaders had increased in large numbers because of the Holy Scriptures which they read, and gave them determination to free the whole of Europe from people who never followed the laws and teachings of Jesus Christ. Basically in religion, creeds and scriptures are the bases of ancient and modern beliefs.

Entertainment too has been greatly transformed because of modern means of communication. Today we have televisions, radios, computers and cinemas which bring visual and audio enjoyment closer to us, unlike in the past where festivals and theaters were meant for only the kings, queens and other high-class people in the society. We all have to say thank you to communication for it has really changed the life of misery and sadness to a life of joy and happiness.

BIBLIOGRAPHY

Lee Richardson (1969). Dimensions of Communication. New York, Louisiana State University, 1969.

Warren K. Agee, Philip H. Ault and Edwin Emery (1988). Introduction to mass Communications. Ninth edition. New York, University of Georgia, South Bend Tribune and University of Minnesota, 1988.